ht © 1984 Leméac Editeur
ion copyright © 1991 John Van Burek and Bill Glassco

ed with assistance from the Canada Council

oks
19 East Cordova Street
ver, British Columbia
V6A 1M8

ok was typeset in Century Oldstyle by Pièce de Résistance Ltée.,
ted and bound in Canada by Hignell Printing Ltd.

vised printing: September 1991

ian Cataloguing in Publication Data

lay, Michel, 1942—
osanna. English]
sanna

play.
anslation of: Hosanna
BN 0-88922-296-7

Title. II. Title: Hosanna. English
.R47H613 1991   C842'.54   C91-091565-2
9.2.T73H613 1991

HOSANNA

Hosar

by Michel Tre

translated by John Van Bur

cop
tra

pub

Tal
201
Van
Can

This
and

First

Right
group
perso
ciés,

Cana

Trem
[
H

A
T
I

I.
PS85
PQ39

Talonbooks   •   Vancou

CHARACTERS:
HOSANNA
CUIRETTE

Hosanna was first performed at le Théâtre de Quat'Sous in Montréal, Québec, on May 10, 1973, with the following cast:

Hosanna   Jean Archambault
Cuirette   Gilles Renaud
                Directed by André Brassard
                Costumes by François Laplante
                Set Design by Paul Buissonneau

Hosanna was first performed in English at Tarragon Theatre in Toronto, Ontario on May 15, 1974, with the following cast:

Hosanna   Richard Monette
Cuirette   Richard Donat
                Directed by Bill Glassco
                Set Design and Costumes by John Ferguson
                Lighting by Vladimir Svetlovsky

The same production opened on Broadway at the Bijou Theatre on October 14, 1974.

This revised English translation of *Hosanna* was first performed at Tarragon Theatre in Toronto, Ontario on May 27, 1987, with the following cast:

Hosanna   Geordie Johnson
Cuirette   Dennis O'Connor
                Directed by Richard Monette
                Set Design and Costumes by Michael Goodwin
                Lighting by Steven Hawkins

- *ACT ONE* -

A "furnished bachelor," somewhere in Plaza Saint-Hubert. A single room comprising living room, bedroom, and an off-stage kitchenette. A sofa-bed, a coffee table, a small bookcase, a bedside table with an enormous urn-lamp, a portable record player, a portable television, a portable radio: in other words, everything that naturally encumbers "bachelor" apartments, which are only so called because no one is honest enough to call them "one-room expensive dumps." It is an atmosphere of sadness and solitude.

The only personal touches in this depressing set are: (1) on the coffee table an awful plaster imitation of "David," as deformed and grotesque as one could imagine, too big for the table, and always in the way of people in the apartment; (2) an "erotic" painting, the work of CUIRETTE, from the days when he had artistic aspirations, hung over the sofa-bed, but unframed; (3) a vanity table, surmounted by a huge mirror, covered with innumerable pots of cream, lipstick, brushes and bottles of all sizes and colours; and (4) an enormous bottle of eau de cologne. (It is important that throughout the play, the audience be able to smell HOSANNA's perfume; a cheap, heavy, disgusting perfume, a perfume so strong that it smells of stuffiness, a perfume that has imprisoned HOSANNA for years, and which leaves rather sickening traces wherever she goes.)

*Through the window, every five seconds, inexorably, the
neon sign from the "Pharmacie Beaubien" flashes on
and off.*

*The phosphorescent alarm clock dial reads three o'clock
(A.M.)*

*HOSANNA comes in very slowly, making no noise.
She stands in the dark for a very long time, without
moving. We hear her breathing, as if she were drinking
the air of her apartment.*

*She can barely be seen in the flashing light of the neon
sign. She should give the appearance of a bundle of rags
that is somehow standing up.*

HOSANNA:
I knew I shouldn't have gone. I knew it . . . I knew
it . . . .

*She goes over to the urn-lamp and lights it. HOSANNA
is a transvestite dressed up as Elizabeth Taylor playing
"Cleopatra," but infinitely more cheap. A Cleopatra-of-
the-streets. Her dress is in wine-red lace, heavily
decorated in gold lace "in the style of the times." The
wig is "real hair." Her sandals come directly from
Park Avenue (Montreal), and the generous portion of
jewels, necklaces, chains, rings, pins, and the cobra
hairpiece that HOSANNA-Cleopatra is wearing, and
the serpents entwined around her arms, all come from
any or several of the 5 & 10 cent stores, or the
"jewellery" shops that line la rue Sainte-Catherine
between Amherst and Saint-Laurent. But despite this
grotesque get-up, CLAUDE-HOSANNA-Cleopatra
should not appear "funny." She is a cheap transvestite,
touching and sad, exasperating in her self-exaltation.*

8

HOSANNA stands for some time next to the urn-lamp.
She looks in the mirror over the vanity table.

HOSANNA:
I knew it. I knew it . . . I should never have gone in
there.

*She approaches the mirror and looks at herself, long
and hard, from head to toe. She looks at herself as one
transvestite looks at another. She starts trembling
slightly.*

*She grabs the bottle of perfume, douses her hands with
the stuff, vigorously rubs them together, then turns
toward the bed-sofa.*

*There, sitting straight up, she begins to cry. With great
difficulty at first, then more and more openly. She never
puts her hands to her face, she doesn't budge, always
sitting very straight, leaning forward ever so slightly.*

HOSANNA:
Stupid bitch! Cheap stupid bitch! Stupid, stupid
bitch . . . .

She calms down, then goes back to the mirror.

That's right, Hosanna. While you're at it, get your face
all streaked. Three hours' work. Half a pound of
sequins! You get one of those in your eyes, you'll have
plenty to cry about. Three hours' work! You stupid bitch.

Silence.

A lifetime, a whole lifetime of preparation and look
where it's got you. Congratulations! Congratulations on
your terrific success!

9

The roar of an old motorcycle is heard arriving outside the house.

Your prince has come, Hosanna. Time to shed your crimson robes!

She takes off her gloves and tries to unhook the dress, but without success.

Shit! I forgot there were hooks. I'm going to get stuck in this thing, I just know it.

A burst of laughter is heard on the stairway. A door slams, and CUIRETTE, in all his splendour, makes his entrance. Of CUIRETTE one would be inclined to say that he is an "old stud." As for the stud, only the costume remains. He is a stud grown old and fat, his leather jacket, once tight and provocative, has been too small for a long time. His old jeans are bulging more with fat than muscles. But as a stud, CUIRETTE has retained his arrogance and easy self-assurance, all of which makes him rather ridiculous sometimes.

CUIRETTE:
"Hosanna, Hosanna, Hosanna, Ho! Hosanna, Hosanna, Hosanna, Ho!" Christ, what a laugh! I never laughed so hard in my life.

He sees HOSANNA.

Well, what do you know, she's back! The Queen of the Nile is already on her throne! Hey, your taxi-driver must have been scared shitless, the way he was moving. I bet he just opened the door and dumped you out, like a bag of dirty laundry, eh? I tried to keep up with you, but he was moving so fast, and I was laughing so hard, I couldn't even steer. You know where I wound up? In the middle of Parc Lafontaine. It's not exactly on the way, but what could I do, eh, that's where the bike wanted to take me. Hey, Hosanna, it's been years since I was through there. And you know what those bastards have done? They've put lights up all over the place. It's lit up, bright as day, the whole park. Looks like shit . . . . Jesus Christ, it stinks in here! How many times I gotta tell you, the place smells like a two-bit whore house!

HOSANNA:
> You . . . . What do you know about whores?

CUIRETTE:
> Smells like a fuckin' perfume factory . . . .

HOSANNA:
> I said what do you know about whores? Did you ever get close enough to smell one?

CUIRETTE:
> Big Pauline-de-Joliette smelled like that. I dumped her, remember? Never went near her again. She made me want to puke.

HOSANNA:
> Poor baby. She must have cried her eyes out for a whole thirty seconds. By the way, what was her real name? Wasn't it Paul?

CUIRETTE:
> They're everywhere, Hosanna, everywhere. There isn't one lousy corner that's not lit up. How can you get any action in a place like that, eh? Christ, they even put in a zoo for the kids!;

HOSANNA:
    It's been there for fifteen years.

CUIRETTE:
    And a theatre too . . . I drove right up to it on my
    bike . . . . All lit up, just like the rest. Lights
    everywhere. Jesus, you can't even get a decent blow-
    job anymore. Not a corner left in the park, Hosanna. I
    tell you, everything's changed. To get a good blowjob
    these days, you gotta find yourself a two-bit whore in a
    cheap perfume factory.

    He laughs.

HOSANNA:
    Okay, Cuirette, you've had a lot to drink tonight, and I
    think we'd better go to bed. When you can't even
    remember there's a zoo and a theatre in the Parc
    Lafontaine, it's time to go to bed. We can talk about
    your perfume in the morning. Right now your two-bit
    whore has had about all she can take.

CUIRETTE:
    Smells like somebody died in here.

    He laughs.

    Hey, you know, when my Uncle Gratien kicked the
    bucket, the funeral parlour stunk like this. I remember
    my Aunt Germaine climbing into the casket screaming,
    "Don't leave me, Gratien, don't leave me!"

HOSANNA:
    I know, I know, and the lid of the coffin fell on her head.
    You've only told me three hundred times. Three
    hundred times you've told me that story.

CUIRETTE:
You don't think it's funny? Pow! Right on the head. And
then you know what she says? "Oh yes, dear, yes, if
you want me to follow you, I will. I'm coming with you,
Gratien, I'm coming!" Christ, that was funny! And your
room, Hosanna, reminds me of my Uncle Gratien's
funeral, and my Aunt Germaine. That's why I'm talking
about it.

HOSANNA:
It's also because you've got nothing else to say . . . .

CUIRETTE:
I said to myself: "Cuirette, my friend, they've built a
theatre on the very spot you made your debut." . . . .
That's not bad, eh? . . . . Not bad at all . . . .

HOSANNA:
Yeah, and one day they're going to tear down the Bijou
Theatre, which is where you're going to end up, and they're
going to build a park in its place . . . . A nice big park
with lots and lots of toilets . . . le Parc Raymond-Cuirette!

CUIRETTE:
Goddamn lights, they're everywhere. They've ruined it,
Hosanna, they've ruined my beautiful park. I started
busting streetlights, but then I stopped 'cause they were
the old ones, and the old ones look kinda nice. You can't
bust the new ones, they're too high. It looks like a
baseball field, for Chrissake!

HOSANNA:
Too bad it wasn't that bright when I met you, eh?

CUIRETTE:
Hey, did you check out the taxi-driver? Whose type was
he, yours or mine?

13

HOSANNA:
>Fat chance he'd be yours, Cuirette. Taxi-drivers dressed as women aren't that easy to come by. Even on Halloween.

CUIRETTE:
>Some of them are women . . . .

HOSANNA:
>Real ones, yes, I know, stupid! It's not the first time I've taken a taxi.

CUIRETTE:
>Yeah, but never that fast. Man, I've never seen you in such a flap.

HOSANNA:
>I wasn't in a flap.

CUIRETTE:
>You want to bet?
HOSANNA:
>I wasn't in a flap, stupid!

CUIRETTE:
>Sure, you kept your dignity till you got to the door. But as soon as they couldn't see you anymore you tore down those stairs like a bat out of hell. And this time you weren't too choosy about whose taxi you got into, eh? You didn't stand there wiggling your ass and giving them the eye, did you? No, you grabbed the first one that came along and you jumped in before the poor bastard knew what hit him. All he saw was a flash of red rags and scrap metal falling into his back seat, and someone screaming, "Get me out of here, get me out of here. I'll tell you where I'm going in a minute."

HOSANNA goes up to CUIRETTE and turns her back to him.

HOSANNA:
Will you unhook my dress?

CUIRETTE:
If it takes as long to get out of it as it did to get in you may as well leave it on till next Halloween.

HOSANNA:
Listen, smarty-pants, if you don't want to do it, just say so and I'll do it myself . . . I can do it myself, you know, if you don't want to help me.

CUIRETTE:
No, no, I'll do it . . . .

The phone rings. CUIRETTE grabs it before undoing even one hook.

Hello? . . . .

Disappointed.

. . . . Oh . . . . Yeah . . . .

to HOSANNA

. . . . It's for you . . . .

HOSANNA:
At this hour? Who is it?

CUIRETTE:
I don't know . . . I don't recognize her voice . . . .

15

HOSANNA:
It's a woman?

CUIRETTE:
I doubt it, but whoever she is, I don't know her.

He starts laughing.

Well, here, see for yourself.

HOSANNA takes the receiver.

HOSANNA:
. . . . Hello . . . .

She stands fixed for a moment, then slams down the receiver and throws the phone on the floor.

CUIRETTE:
So, did you know her?

HOSANNA:
Fat bitch!

CUIRETTE:
Listen, baby, I've already told you. I'm not one of the girls.

HOSANNA:
I wasn't talking about you . . . . You're not so important that I talk about you all the time. You're not that important! Besides, in that idiot outfit you look so little like a man, if anyone heard me calling you a bitch they'd take you for a lesbian!

CUIRETTE:
Yeah. Well, I'm no lesbian, and I can prove it.

HOSANNA:
You? You couldn't prove a goddamn thing. You don't got what it takes.

CUIRETTE:
You want the proof, Hosanna?

HOSANNA:
No thanks. I've swallowed enough for one night!

CUIRETTE:
You're too much, you know that? Swallowed enough for one night. You really know how to dish it out, don't you? I'll bet your customers lap it right up when you talk like that.

HOSANNA:
Oh, sure, I'm the funniest hairdresser in town . . . .

HOSANNA picks up the telephone, hesitates before putting it in place, then does so.

And I'm very, very popular with the Jewish ladies because I don't singe their hair . . . . Funny and clever! The secret of my success.

CUIRETTE:
Does my Queen-of-the-Nile hairdresser still want to get unhooked?

The telephone rings again, and HOSANNA grabs it right away.

HOSANNA:
> Go shit yourself, Sandra! Go shit yourself, you dried up cunt!

She hangs up.

CUIRETTE:
> You were hoping she'd phone back, weren't you ?

HOSANNA:
> And you recognized her voice, didn't you?

CUIRETTE:
> No. Anyway, I don't think it was her. She probably got somebody else to do it.

HOSANNA:
> You knew goddamn well she was gonna phone. Another one of your stupid jokes!

CUIRETTE:
> No . . . .

HOSANNA:
> Yes! Every chance you get, you . . . .

The phone rings.

HOSANNA:
> Goddamn it, what's she calling for? What the hell does she want? Is she going to keep calling all night?

CUIRETTE answers the phone.

CUIRETTE:
> Hello, Sandra? Is that you, Sandra? Hello! Okay, that's enough. It was funny the first time, but . . . .

18

A moment, then CUIRETTE starts to laugh.

CUIRETTE:

Yeah, sure, but listen, put yourself in her place . . . .

HOSANNA:

Don't worry, she's been trying to do that for four
years, the bitch!

CUIRETTE:

Alright, Sandra, the party's over . . . . It was lots of
fun, but leave Hosanna alone now, okay?

HOSANNA:

Oh, so you're siding with me now? That really takes
the cake!

CUIRETTE:

Naw, I don't feel like it . . . I'm going to stay here.

HOSANNA:

You're goddamn right you're going to stay here . . . .

She grabs the phone away from CUIRETTE.

Hello, Sandra, how are you, dear? I'm fine, thank you,
but listen, it's three-thirty and I have to go to work
tomorrow, so if you don't mind I'd like to go to bed,
okay? It's nice of you to invite Cuirette to spend the
night, but Cuirette is my husband and he's going to
stay here. And Sandra, you've been chasing him a long
time, and all the time he's been laughing in your face,
so it's time you realized he's not the least bit
interested in you, in fact, you give us both the shits!
Oh, you were very funny tonight, and you were very
pleased that everyone laughed at your stupid jokes, but
too bad you didn't notice how they laughed even harder

19

every time you turned your back, eh, because your dress was so tight you split a seam and one of your magnificent rolls of fat was sticking out like a big pink sausage. And what's more, Sandra, there's nothing so ugly in this world as a real yellow dress on a dyed blond!

She hangs up.

CUIRETTE:
What a mouth!

HOSANNA:
I must remember that the next time I use it on you, Rosa . . . . Excuse me! Rosario!

CUIRETTE:
Water off a duck's back, baby . . . .

HOSANNA:
Yes, but it's a long time since you lost your feathers, ducky. And if there's anyone who's not waterproof, it's you! Come on, unhook me, and let's go to bed.

CUIRETTE:
I don't feel like it . . . .

HOSANNA stares at CUIRETTE for a long moment.

HOSANNA:
You don't feel like what . . . . Unhooking me or going to bed?

CUIRETTE:
You've been crying, eh?

HOSANNA suddenly starts fighting with her dress.

HOSANNA:
I've been known to do that, yes.

CUIRETTE:
I hadn't noticed . . . I'm sorry.

He goes to help her.

HOSANNA:
What do you want, five bucks?

CUIRETTE:
I've had better offers.

As if nothing happened.

You ought to just tear it off anyway. I doubt if you'll be wearing it again for a while.

HOSANNA stops struggling.

HOSANNA:
You're right, I won't be wearing it for a while. I won't be wearing it for a long time! But it took me three weeks to make it, and I'm going to keep it.

CUIRETTE:
Sure, hang it in the closet, and everytime you open the door, you can think of tonight and get real sad. Man, you just love to suffer, don't you, you really love to suffer.

HOSANNA doesn't answer, but starts fighting with her dress again.

HOSANNA:

That's one . . . .

CUIRETTE:

There's only a hundred and seventy-nine left . . . . I'm gonna open the window. I just walked by the operating table. If I don't get some air, I'm gonna pass out.

HOSANNA:

Cuirette, please! Open the window, open the door, open the bed, open whatever you want, but for Chrissake, shut your mouth, you're driving me nuts!

CUIRETTE:

You want me to go to Sandra's party? My bike's just outside the door . . . .

HOSANNA:

Go right ahead! And while you're at it, take a ride through the park. You can stop and have a good cry over the scene of your debut, which by the way nobody gives a shit about, even though you bore us all to tears with it . . . . Shit! I've broken a nail. That's the second one tonight! Shit!

CUIRETTE: *opening the window*

I doubt if Cleopatra talked like that . . . .

HOSANNA:

Cleopatra didn't have to undo her own hooks!

CUIRETTE:

Cleopatra didn't have hooks!

CUIRETTE leans on the window sill while HOSANNA continues her dance.

22

HOSANNA:
> If I can just get the first few, the rest will be
> easy . . . . Jesus, I hate it when I break a nail. It
> makes my fingers look all naked . . . . Can't do a
> goddamn thing with it . . . . Gets caught on everything
> too . . . .

CUIRETTE:
> Cats are like that . . . .

HOSANNA:
> What?

CUIRETTE:
> Cats. You know, if you cut a cat's claws . . . .

HOSANNA:
> Oh, I guess I'd better file it. If I don't, it'll just break
> more . . . .

CUIRETTE:
> If you cut their claws, they don't know what to
> do . . . .

HOSANNA:
> Hey, Cuirette, did you take my nail file?

CUIRETTE:
> It's sort of like they're lost . . . . They look
> around . . . . Their eyes big like saucers . . . . Can't
> feel a thing.

HOSANNA:
> Cuirette, for Chrissake, it's not their claws that do
> that, it's their whiskers! That happens when you cut
> their whiskers.

HOSANNA has found her nail file, and starts filing her broken nail.

Long silence.

CUIRETTE looks down the street.

There, that's much better. Goddamn hooks, they always come undone during a smart social evening, and you sit there like a stunned duck trying to look beautiful while everyone laughs at you. But then as soon as you want to undo them . . . .

She struggles with the dress.

. . . . As soon as you want to undo them, they won't budge . . . . They're like padlocks . . . I knew I should have bought snaps!

CUIRETTE: *looking outside*
One of these days, I'm gonna smash that fucker . . . .

HOSANNA:
Who?

CUIRETTE:
Relax, I wasn't talking about you . . . . You're not so important that I talk about you *all* the time . . . . The sign . . . . The Pharmacie Beaubien sign . . . . One of these days I'm gonna smash it. Between that sign and your perfume, this place is the pits!

HOSANNA:
And me? Aren't you forgetting me?

CUIRETTE:
You? You're as bad as the dump you live in. You stink of perfume three blocks away, and most of the time

you're lit up like that goddamn sign. You oughta know
by now, you make me sick . . . .

HOSANNA:
Yes, I know, and I know what you think of the sign and
the perfume . . . . Whew, I've got to stop . . . I'm all
out of breath . . . . If I don't sit down for a minute I'm
going to have mass hysteria . . . . Give me a cigarette.
Hey Cuirette, I'm talking to you! Give me a cigarette!

*CUIRETTE gives HOSANNA a cigarette, and she
places it in a long cigarette-holder. CUIRETTE lights
it for her.*

CUIRETTE:
After your cigarette, you want me to help you with
your dress?

HOSANNA:
No way, Sonny. I've always done everything myself.

CUIRETTE:
Everything?

HOSANNA:
Oh, you're so subtle! Besides, I'm not going to let a
few hooks get me down.

Woman of the world.

That must look chic, eh, a woman with her dress half
undone, drawing voluptuously on a cigarette holder? . . . .

CUIRETTE:
Not a woman who's been working on her hooks for half
an hour and sweating like a pig . . . .

25

HOSANNA:
I'm talking about the overall effect, dummy! It's not
necessary to go into details. Nor do you have to know
what happened before, or what's going to happen
after . . . . Just the overall effect . . . Regarde . . . .

She smokes voluptuously.

CUIRETTE:
Well, baby, the effect you have on me . . . .

HOSANNA:
Oh, go take a shit!

CUIRETTE:
That's your answer to everything, eh? Tell people to go take
a shit.

HOSANNA:
Precisely. It's less complicated. That way you know
where they are and they don't bother you . . . . Oh,
no, tonight I'm just not up to it. The voluptuous,
provocative poses will have to wait . . . . Hey,
wouldn't it be funny if my hooks got stuck in the sofa
and I couldn't get up! "Hosanna is dead, pinned to her
sofa like a rare and precious butterfly."

CUIRETTE:
See, you're in better mood already!

HOSANNA:
Like hell. If your hooks got stuck, you might develop a
sense of humour too. It's called "trying to forget." Or
is that too subtle for you?

CUIRETTE:
So, are we gonna have a second round, or aren't we?

"Ladies and Gentlemen, presenting 'Hosanna-of-the-Hooks,' a new and exotic number executed by - and when I say executed, Ladies and Gentlemen, I mean executed- by the tantalizing, the seductive, the show-stopping one-and-only Hosanna, Hosanna, Hosanna, Ho!

HOSANNA lunges at CUIRETTE and puts out her cigarette on his forehead.

Hey, you fucking maniac!

HOSANNA:
Don't you ever say that again, Cuirette, you hear me? Never! I've put up with a lot for a long time but I never want to hear you say that again as long as you live! Can't you see I'm trying not to think about it? Not another word about tonight, not another word!

CUIRETTE runs to the kitchen and opens the refrigerator. He takes out the butter and rubs some on his forehead.

That's right, do like Mommy said. When we get a little burn we put some butter on it and the hurt goes away all by itself . . . .

CUIRETTE:
Crazy bitch! You could have put my eye out.

HOSANNA:
No way Jose. I knew where I was aiming. It's bad enough having a husband who's fat, I don't want him half blind as well.

CUIRETTE grabs HOSANNA by the arm.

CUIRETTE:
It's a beating you want, eh? That's what you're looking for.

HOSANNA:
Don't touch me! Take your hands off me!

CUIRETTE:
Well, I'm not going to give you one. Why should I touch you anyway? You like it too much when I touch you. Eh?

HOSANNA: *rubbing her arm*
Didn't even hurt me.

CUIRETTE:
Oh yeah? Try reaching your stupid hooks . . . . Go on, try it. See if I didn't hurt you.

HOSANNA tries to reach her hooks.

HOSANNA:
Ow! Jesus!

CUIRETTE:
Remember the other day? You said I don't have a strong grip anymore?

HOSANNA:
You've got a strong grip for breaking people's arms . . . . But that's all.

CUIRETTE:
Not according to Sandra . . . .

HOSANNA:
Sandra doesn't know what she's talking about, the jealous bitch. All she's done for four years is drool over

28

you. And I don't know why, eh, because there's not much to get excited about. But then, maybe two fatsos together . . . .

CUIRETTE:
What makes you think she doesn't know what she's talking about? Eh?

HOSANNA:
Don't give me any of your fantasies, Cuirette. I don't buy them. You've never been to bed with Sandra and you never will. All you can do is make an ass of yourself whenever she's around.

Suddenly changing her tone.

She'd love to, she'd just love to, but not you.

CUIRETTE:
How do you know?

HOSANNA:
I'd rather not talk about it, I might get nasty . . . . Aw, come on, this has gone on long enough. I'm sick of having this thing on my back . . . . Just undo two or three and I'll do the rest . . . .

HOSANNA turns her back to CUIRETTE, who looks at her for a moment. Slowly, he begins to undo her dress.

CUIRETTE:
You could have put my eye out.

HOSANNA:
I *should* have put your eye out. Nuance.

29

CUIRETTE:
Okay, butterfly, you can climb out of your cocoon now . . . .
Come on, spread your wings, the night air awaits you . . . .

HOSANNA removes her dress. She is wearing panties and a bra.

Silence.

HOSANNA:
Did I really hurt you? Let me see . . . . Bah, it's not so bad . . . . All you can see is butter . . . .

CUIRETTE:
Claude . . . .

HOSANNA turns away brusquely.

HOSANNA:
My name is Hosanna.

CUIRETTE goes back to the window.

HOSANNA speaks to the mirror.

I should have started with the wig. If I'd started with that it would have made more sense . . . . But I don't feel like it . . . I don't feel like taking it off . . . .

CUIRETTE: *out the window*
It's true . . . I am getting fat . . . .

HOSANNA:
What?

CUIRETTE:
I said one of these days I'm gonna smash that fucking sign . . . .

Silence.

HOSANNA:
 I think I'll go to bed with my make-up on,
 Cuirette . . . I'm afraid of what's underneath . . . .

CUIRETTE:
 What?

HOSANNA:
 I said I ought to change my perfume.

CUIRETTE: *turning toward HOSANNA*
 Are you kidding?

HOSANNA:
 Another perfume wouldn't make any difference,
 Cuirette. You'd still choke on it.

CUIRETTE:
 At least it wouldn't be that one . . . .

 HOSANNA grabs the perfume bottle and douses her
 arms and neck. CUIRETTE turns back to the
 window.

HOSANNA: *looking in the mirror*
 Christ, are you stupid!

CUIRETE:
 What?

HOSANNA:
 I was just telling myself how stupid I am . . . .

CUIRETTE:
> You're just finding that out?

HOSANNA:
> Oh, no . . . .

> *CUIRETTE looks outside, HOSANNA looks in the mirror.*

CUIRETTE:
> You can't even see the end of the street . . . .

HOSANNA:
> Cuirette, I'll never move . . . . And I'll never change my perfume.

CUIRETTE:
> You know, we'd be able to see all the way to Bélanger . . . . Look at the stupid thing. On, off, on, off, all night long. Every other sign in town goes off at midnight, but not this one. There are times I see red in my sleep . . . . On, off, on, off, on, off, on, off . . . . He must be crazy, that guy, wasting all that money on electricty . . . . Hell, we're the only ones who ever look at his goddamn sign.

HOSANNA:
> That's right, we're the only ones . . . .

CUIRETTE:
> And it's driving us nuts . . . .

HOSANNA:
> It doesn't bother me . . . . It doesn't bother me in the least. In fact, I'd even go so far as to say that . . . I need it . . . .

CUIRETTE: *turning to HOSANNA*
Need it! What the hell for? What in the name of Christ could . . . .

HOSANNA:
Cuirette, that sign . . . . Oh, never mind . . . . You'd only laugh again . . . .

Silence.

CUIRETTE:
You know, it's funny, seeing you like that . . . .

HOSANNA:
What?

CUIRETTE:
With your make-up on and your dress off . . . . You look funny . . . .

HOSANNA:
But I'm not funny . . . . Not the least bit funny. Not funny at all . . . .

Long pause.

I'm ridiculous.

CUIRETTE: *approaching her*
Come on, I don't think so . . . .

HOSANNA:
When I'm dressed like a man, I'm ridiculous. When I'm dressed like a woman, I'm ridiculous. But I'm really ridiculous when I'm stuck between the two, like I am right now, with my woman's face, my woman's underwear, and my own body . . . .

CUIRETTE: *putting his hand on her shoulders*
I don't think you're ridiculous . . . .

HOSANNA: *very softly, suddenly very tired*
Raymond, please, don't touch me . . . .

CUIRETTE:
Don't worry, I wasn't planning to . . . . The smell
doesn't exactly turn me on . . .

HOSANNA throws her perfume bottle and breaks it.

HOSANNA:
There, now it's really gonna stink! Go ahead, have
your fit!

CUIRETTE:
It's not me who wants to have a fit, Claude, it's you!
But you're trying to keep it in, aren't you? You're
trying to keep it in, but it's not going to work. And as
for your fucking perfume, I've put up with it for four
goddamn years, so it's not about to kill me now. Not
even a gallon of it!

HOSANNA:
Then why do you always talk about it!

CUIRETTE:
Because, as you told me a few minutes ago,
sweetheart, I got nothing else to say!

HOSANNA coughs.

There, you see, you're choking on it yourself. I told
you it stinks in here. I better clean it up right now
'cause I know you won't do it, and if you cut yourself
it'll be all my fault.

HOSANNA gets up and goes to the window.

That's right, see if you can see Bélanger.

He bends down to pick up the broken glass.

And if you're gonna be sick, do it in the bathroom.
Christ, it stinks so bad in here we're gonna wake up
the neighbours . . .

He picks up her dress and hangs it in the closet.

So . . . into the closet with the Queen of the Nile, until
her next appearance in society . . . . Hey, Hosanna, if
you were to die all of a sudden, I think I'd have you
embalmed in this thing!

HOSANNA does not even react.

I can see it now . . . . The look on people's
faces . . . . Especially your old lady . . . even for this I
bet she'd have an explanation. "Don't be ridiculous,
my dear, that's not a dress, it's . . . just a fancy shirt.
He was a very imaginative boy, you know, very
creative." Man, I bet Sandra'd get a charge out of
that, eh?

Silence.

I hung your dress in the middle of the closet. So every
time you open the door it'll stare you right in the face,
and you can suffer, baby, suffer . . . .

HOSANNA still does not react.

I'm going to make the bed . . . .

HOSANNA:
Usually it's freezing on Halloween.

CUIRETTE passes in front of the vanity mirror.

CUIRETTE:
That's what you should have busted . . . .

HOSANNA:
Not in a hundred years . . . . It's a souvenir . . . . Like everything else.

CUIRETTE:
How do you know what I'm talking about?

HOSANNA: *very softly*
You just said you were going to make the bed, Cuirette. As soon as you say that, I know everything you're going to do next . . . Every night for four years you've done exactly the same thing. I don't even need to watch. That's how I know you just passed in front of the mirror . . . .

CUIRETTE moves the coffee table from in front of the sofa, and starts to open the bed.

And when you start to open up the bed, it's going to get stuck and you're going to say "shit" . . . .

CUIRETTE:
Shit!

HOSANNA shrugs her shoulders.

HOSANNA:
Then you're going to ask me, "When are we going to get rid of this thing?"

36

CUIRETTE:
When are we going to get rid of this thing?

HOSANNA:
And I'm going to answer . . .

She turns toward CUIRETTE.

When you start working, Raymond, when you start
working.

She looks back out the window.

Would you mind telling me what difference it would
make if we could see all the way to Bélanger? There's
probably another sign blocking the view anyway.

CUIRETTE:
At least we wouldn't have that mother staring at us all
the time. Oops, I almost knocked old David on his ass!

HOSANNA:
Well, I think it's just fine, that sign . . . just fine . . . .
We should leave the window open tonight. Just think,
it's November, that's really amazing. It's almost warm.

CUIRETTE:
Yeah, and we'll be paying for it in January, you
wait . . . . The bed's ready . . . .

HOSANNA:
No, not going to bed yet . . . not tired . . . .

CUIRETTE:
You're working tomorrow . . . . It's Saturday, your
heaviest day . . . .

HOSANNA:

No, not going in . . . . Besides, I won't sleep
now . . . .

CUIRETTE starts to get undressed.

You go to bed . . . . The sign'll go off any minute
now . . . . It must be nearly four . . . . You'd think it
would be chilly, eh . . . I can't understand it . . . .

*Before he gets into bed, CUIRETTE looks at his
erotic painting over the sofa.*

CUIRETTE:

I wonder if I could still sell my painting. That'd give me
some bread for a while.

HOSANNA:

Dreamer! Anyway, it's not yours to sell. You gave it to
me. Besides, no one else would be sucker enough to
hang that thing over their bed.

CUIRETTE:

It's not half as bad as the crap they sell down at Place
Ville-Marie. Maybe I oughta take it up again . . . .

HOSANNA:

I'd say it makes up for the sign and the perfume. Hey,
Picasso, did you ever think of that? Maybe your
painting doesn't smell, but Christ, it's ugly! It's as hard
to stomach as my perfume.

CUIRETTE:

I think about it a lot sometimes . . . I don't know . . . .
Maybe I will . . . .

HOSANNA: *still looking outside*
Look, make you a deal . . . I'll take down the painting,
and you can take down the sign . . . .

CUIRETTE:
It'd be nice to get back into that . . . .

HOSANNA:
Then we'll hang the sign in here, and the painting
outside . . . . The pharmacy will go bankrupt, and I'll
get to keep the sign . . . .

CUIRETTE:
I don't know if I could still do it though . . . I was
pretty good in those days, you know, but for stuff like
that it takes of lot of . . . concentration.

HOSANNA:
In that case, you'd better forget it.

CUIRETTE:
Oh well, I'm going to bed . . .

The phone rings.

HOSANNA:
If that's Sandra, tell her that besides being ugly, her
dress was so short you could see her tampax sticking
out . . . .

CUIRETTE:
She was wearing a long dress . . . . Hello . . . .

HOSANNA:
I know she was wearing a long dress, stupid!

CUIRETTE:
Yeah . . . .

HOSANNA:
Tell her that her tampax was sticking out anyway. She had a long, long string on it.

CUIRETTE:
Ah . . . . No.

HOSANNA:
Is it her?

CUIRETTE:
Yeah, but don't make it any earlier . . .

HOSANNA:
Who is it?

CUIRETTE:
Oh no, we're not changing that . . . .

HOSANNA:
Cuirette, who is it? Is it Sandra?

CUIRETTE:
Will you shut up! It's for me.

HOSANNA:
Oh, la, la, I beg your pardon . . . I understand, I understand. Excuse me, my lord . . . I'll just withdraw into my apartments . . . . For once I'll tell myself to take a shit!

She goes into the bathroom.

CUIRETTE:
Hi . . . . I didn't think you were gonna call. I was getting ready to go to bed . . . .

He laughs.

Hell no, I never do that by myself . . . . Only when I'm desperate.

Laughs again.

Yeah, as a matter of fact, she phoned a while ago to invite me . . . . What do you think, is there gonna be any action? . . . . Okay, great, I'll see you there. Oh, hey, you really missed something tonight . . . . Did you hear about it?

HOSANNA comes out of the bathroom.

Don't worry, she doesn't scare me . . . .

Seeing HOSANNA.

Yeah, sure, we'll . . . keep in touch . . . . See ya.

He hangs up.

HOSANNA:
Did you ever see a woman pee standing up? . . . . I was watching myself in the mirror . . . Elizabeth Taylor, standing in profile, with this thing hanging out . . . pissing . . . . Disgusting.

Pause.

Who phoned? Some new snatch?

CUIRETTE:
Why do you say it like that?

HOSANNA:
Christ, you don't expect me to call them your
girlfriends, do you?

CUIRETTE:
Yeah, it was some new snatch.

HOSANNA:
For tonight?

CUIRETTE:
Yep!

HOSANNA:
Just like that, at four in the morning! I suppose that
was arranged in advance, like everything else tonight!

Trying to be funny.

HOSANNA:
Oh, I'd better close the window, eh? . . . . You never
know what might happen . . . . A young girl, all alone
in the house . . . . Ha, ha, ha. Aren't I funny? Oh well,
I suppose the best thing that could happen to me
tonight just isn't going to happen . . . .

She lets herself fall on the bed.

CUIRETTE: *after a moment*
You want me to stay?

HOSANNA:
No, I don't want you to stay . . . I need you to stay,
but I don't *want* you to . . . . Anything I might need
doesn't matter anyway . . . . Go on, go out and get
laid, it'll do us both some good. You and your big dick, me
and my little pea-brain.

CUIRETTE:
Who said anything about getting laid? I'm just going to a party at Sandra's . . . .

HOSANNA:
Jesus, are you naive! Sometimes I think you make a point of being stupid. You know perfectly well how Sandra's parties turn out. They're worse than a goddamn Fellini movie, for Chrissake! She must spend the next three days just getting the place picked up . . . . Picking herself up too, eh, or rather coming back down, after all the speed she takes . . . And I'm warning you, eh, don't come home all speeded up like last time. For three days you looked like a glass of Bromo Seltzer.

CUIRETTE:
I felt like one too . . . . It was great . . . .

HOSANNA:
Yeah, sure, you were having a ball, but for me it was a pain in the ass . . . . It's all very well to feel like a Bromo, Cuirette, but when you've been fizzing for fourteen hours, I'd settle for indigestion!

CUIRETTE:
What do you know about it, you farmer? You never tried anything.

HOSANNA:
Cuirette, just watching you come down tells me a lot about your phony paradise . . . .

CUIRETTE:
Chicken shit . . . .

CUIRETTE starts getting dressed again.

43

HOSANNA:

Maybe so. But if you could see yourself after you've been shooting up, you'd be chicken too.

CUIRETTE:

Who cares what you look like, it's what you feel that counts . . . .

HOSANNA:

Will you listen to her . . . I can "feel" things without that, thank you.

CUIRETTE:

You stupid twat! You never understand a thing!

HOSANNA:

Tell me, were you taking drugs . . . .

CUIRETTE:

Drugs!

HOSANNA:

. . . . Back in your purple shit phase, were you taking drugs then? No! Are you still painting that purple shit today? No! What you were doing, Cuirette, was really ugly, but my God, at least it was something!

CUIRETTE:

What I take has nothing to do with . . . . Man, you really know how to twist things, don't you!

HOSANNA:

Listen, the day you found out your stuff wasn't worth shit you didn't feel so good then, did you? You told me so yourself. You took acid, you looked at your paintings, and pouff, you couldn't create anymore.

CUIRETTE:
Anyone can have bad trips . . . .

HOSANNA:
No, no, no, you don't take bad trips if you don't know how to handle them.

CUIRETTE:
Which means *you* don't know how to handle them.

HOSANNA:
That's right, and I'm not afraid to admit it . . . . What if I'd been stoned tonight?

CUIRETTE:
Wow! I never thought of that. Would have been even funnier. Oh yeah, I can just see it!

HOSANNA:
On the other hand, that might have saved me . . . . It might have kept me from going up on that stage . . . .

Pause.

So, you're off to Sandra's, are you? Who is she, by the way . . . your latest heart throb?

CUIRETTE: You don't know her . . . .

HOSANNA:
I know everyone who's gay in Montreal, my dear, even the ones who don't know it themselves. Unless of course she's fresh in from Drummondville, and I haven't had the pleasure of meeting her on the circuit . . . yet. Can't you at least tell me her name?

CUIRETTE:
>   Reynald.

HOSANNA:
>   Reynald! She hasn't even taken a maiden name, and
>   you're interested in him already! Is he nice and lady-
>   like at least?

CUIRETTE:
>   I don't know if he's "nice and lady-like," but he's a lot
>   better-looking than you!

HOSANNA:
>   Well, my beauty, that's not so hard. Can't you do
>   better than that?

>   *She goes over to her vanity table and sits down. She
>   takes the pot of cold cream.*

>   No . . . . No, I just can't do it . . . . That reminds me,
>   lover boy, while you're out dancing a fugue with your
>   new nymphette, see if you can arrange to stay away
>   for a few days. My mother's arriving tomorrow, I
>   forgot to tell you . . . there's only room for two in this
>   place, and since it's my bed and my apartment . . . .

CUIRETTE:
>   You cocksucker!

HOSANNA:
>   Watch your language, dear, you're getting vulgar. Since
>   you've been putting on weight you have a tendency to
>   get gross.

>   *Pause.*

>   You should be happy . . . . Everything's working out
>   fine . . . . You'd have had to go anyway . . . . Look,

take Reynalda on a little honeymoon, why don't you?
Then, when the fun's over . . . if you feel like it . . . .

Defeated, HOSANNA stops suddenly.

Very low.

You're right, it stinks in here. And it's not the perfume
either . . . .

CUIRETTE:
I don't believe you. It's not true your mother's coming
tomorrow.

HOSANNA:
Oh yes, it is. It certainly is . . . .

CUIRETTE:
You're just saying that to fuck me around . . . .

HOSANNA:
She phoned the day before yesterday . . . or was it
yesterday? . . . . Anyway, she phoned . . . .

CUIRETTE:
You know I don't have a cent. You know I got no place
to go . . . I don't believe you . . . .

HOSANNA: *shouting*
Then don't believe me, goddamn it, but don't come
back for three days, that's all!

CUIRETTE:
I don't have to do whatever you say, you know . . . .

HOSANNA:
When it's me who's paying the rent, you do! Now

listen, stud, you're going to that party! I'm telling you to go because I need my apartment. You can sleep wherever you like and with whomever you like, I don't give a shit, but I don't want my mother to walk in here and find you, is that clear, Einstein? I'm supposed to be living alone, see, so I don't want to get caught making out with some has-been motorcycle freak whose greatest disappointment in life was that he never got to be Marlon Brando's understudy!

CUIRETTE:

What difference would it make? She's seen others, even though she pretended not to! Anyway, she's seen me . . . .

HOSANNA:

My mother doesn't know I'm the way I am, and . . . .

CUIRETTE:

For Chrissake, Hosanna, you can smell your fuckin' perfume down on the street! All you gotta do is walk by, and you know there's a queer living in the place. You can find the right apartment by just following your nose! Besides, it's a waste of time hiding all your wigs, your gowns, your high-heels, your big sexy David there . . . . Your old lady never sees 'em anyway. The last time she popped in from Ste-Eustache, remember that, "Surprise, surprise?" I was here then, I saw how you two carried on. We'd just finished supper, eh? I was getting ready to do the dishes, and you were putting on your make-up, remember, 'cause you were going out that night. In fact, you were putting on your make-up when she walked in the door, Hosanna. You didn't have time to turn your stinkbox here into a "straight" apartment, did you? The whole time she was here, she pretended to see nothing. Not a goddamn thing! After she kissed you she had to take a kleenex and wipe her mouth 'cause you had pancake all over your face. But she didn't say a word . . . . And all the time you were farting around in the closet looking for the "basic black number" you were supposed to wear that night, you know where it was? Draped over the only goddamn chair your mother could have sat down in! Still, not a word. Even when I shouted, "Has the mother-in-law arrived?" she didn't hear a thing. Nothing! I did it on purpose too, just to see what she'd do. When you introduced me to her, I had a frying pan in one hand, a dish towel in the other, and an apron around my waist. And I don't exactly look like a maid, do I, Hosanna! "How do you do," she says in her nice polite voice, but she was looking three feet off to the side . . . . She only looked at me once . . . I got up to take some things out to the kitchen, and when I came back I knew she'd been checking me out 'cause all of a sudden she looked away. And right there, she gave you this sign of approval! Yeah, Hosanna, approval! . . . . As if to say, "He's very nice, Claude. Your friend is very nice. I approve . . . ." So, if it's really true she's coming here tomorrow, and she finds me sleeping in your bed, she's gonna tell you the same thing, Claude, the same thing, "Your friend is very nice. I approve."

HOSANNA:
You're wrong, Cuirette. She won't tell me the same thing.

CUIRETTE:
You're fuckin' sick, the two of you.

HOSANNA:
Besides, there's not much left to approve, so why disappoint her?

CUIRETTE:

Well, at least you admit she knows . . . .

HOSANNA:

Okay, okay, she knows, she knows. So what!

CUIRETTE:

So why do you two keep playing games? Why's she pretend she doesn't know?

HOSANNA:

We talked about it once, Cuirette, and that was enough.

CUIRETTE:

And I suppose you got it all straightened out, just like that . . . .

HOSANNA:

I'm the one who doesn't want to talk about it.

CUIRETTE:

Huh?

HOSANNA:

Look, you're all dressed, you're ready to go out, so go. Go, Raymond. Go to your fucking party . . . .

HOSANNA gets up and goes towards the window.

Me, I'll wave goodbye with my big white hanky.

CUIRETTE:

One of the biggest queens in Montreal, and you can't even talk about it with your old lady.

HOSANNA:

One of the biggest queens, are you blind? Not after tonight, I'm not. As for my old lady, sweetheart, I'm not afraid to talk to her about anything . . . . It's getting cold . . . . It's almost light . . . . And I'm standing here without a stitch.

HOSANNA closes the window and goes to the closet. The first thing she sees, obviously, is the Cleopatra dress.

Oh, you put it in a good place, that's for sure.

She takes a dressing gown and puts it on.

You want to know what she said when she found out I was gay? Huh? You want to know? I was in grade seven at Ste-Eustache, and they used to laugh at me because I looked so much like a girl . . . . Don't worry, Cuirette, this won't take long. I'm not a masochist. Besides, it makes no difference what they did to me, at least I got out. Which is more than I can say for the jerks in my class who were always feeling me up and writing "Lemieux's a queer" all over the johns. "Lemieux wants your hard on, so be hard on Lemieux" . . . . No, I don't think about it much anymore. They were just a bunch of sick perverts anyway . . . . But her . . . . What *she* did to me, that's another story.

Silence.

She must have known long before I told her. Christ, everyone else knew. Which is to say, everyone had decided. They'd seen it, they'd figured it out, they talked about it, and they all thought it was very funny. When I realized the truth . . . . When I saw that to be queer doesn't just mean that you act like a girl, but can also mean you really want to be a girl, a real girl, and that you can manage to become one . . . . Christ, you can actually manage to become a real girl . . . . When I realized it was true, that the guys in my school, especially the older ones in the ninth grade . . . attracted me . . . I went straight to my mother. Jesus, how's that for being stupid! I was naive enough to think that . . . she'd help me . . . or at least explain it to me . . . what it all meant . . . . My mother, who'd always kissed me and pampered me, and dressed me up, who never stopped telling me how dangerous women were and that I shouldn't go near them . . . because she wanted to keep me all to herself . . . to be her crutch in her old age, she said . . . . She was scared that some woman would come and steal me . . . . Bullshit! . . . . You know what she said to me when I told her I'd begun to sleep with men? She said, "If that's the way you want to be, Claude, just make sure they're good-looking." That was it. Not another word. And she figured she could hold on to me.

Silence.

But the day I turned sixteen I was on my way to Montreal with the first trick I could lay my hands on. And then . . . step by step . . . little by little . . . I became Hosanna . . . Hosanna, the biker's girlfriend! Hosanna, the stud's favourite hairdresser! Hosanna, the motorcycle queen! And ever since then, whenever she and I get together, we act like nothing's happened. She pretends she doesn't see a thing so she won't have to talk about it. As for me, I have no wish to entertain her with my "great erotic escapades." So there you are. That's it. The end of this touching and most unoriginal success story . . . . So touching, and so second-rate . . . .

52

CUIRETTE:
How come you never told me that before?

HOSANNA:
Raymond, there are times I hate that woman so much I
don't know what to do to her, I don't know what. I
was hoping I'd win tonight, because if I had, every
paper in the city would have had my picture in it, and
underneath my real name . . . I would have insisted on
my real name, Cuirette . . . because that just might
have killed her, the bitch!

CUIRETTE:
How come you never told me . . . .

HOSANNA:
What difference would that have made? . . . . I don't
need anyone's pity . . . .

CUIRETTE:
You really are stupid. Why are you telling me now, for
Chrissake! Just to keep me here longer?

HOSANNA:
To keep you here . . . . Who do you think you are?
You could have walked out anytime, Cuirette. Besides,
I wasn't talking to you . . . .

CUIRETTE:
Fine, so go ahead and talk to yourself . . . .

He goes towards the door.

HOSANNA: *without looking at him*
By the way, you shouldn't wear your belt too tight.

CUIRETTE:
> What?

HOSANNA:
> Your belt, it's too tight, dear . . . . Your rolls are
> hanging out.

> *CUIRETTE looks at his belly.*

HOSANNA:
> You'll never turn Reynalda on with all that sticking out
> over the top of your pants . . . . Not unless she goes
> for fatsos . . .

> *CUIRETTE comes back towards HOSANNA.*

CUIRETTE:
> Look, I told you . . . .

HOSANNA: *cutting him off*
> I've been watching you get fat, Cuirette! You're fatter
> now than you were last week, and next week you'll be
> fatter still. If you go on eating like a pig and drinking
> beer like a fish, you'll split your pants and pop all
> your buttons.

CUIRETTE:
> That's not true!

> *CUIRETTE adjusts his pants.*

HOSANNA:
> You're not what you used to be, Raymond . . . .

CUIRETTE:
> Alright, alright, I know, I'm not what I used to
> be . . . I'm fat . . . okay? I have a tough time getting

into my pants, and I got no money to buy a new pair . . . okay? I know all that, Hosanna, every bit of it. I was good-looking once, damn good-looking, and now I'm not anymore. And I also know why you're always reminding me of it. It's because maybe, just *maybe* it helps you forget that you're getting old and ugly yourself. Yeah, that's right. When it comes to getting old, Hosanna, you're getting there fast . . . . But your problem isn't around your belly, sweetheart, it's in your face!

HOSANNA:

If you don't shut your mouth . . . .

CUIRETTE:

You just love to laugh at other people's faults. That's all you ever do is laugh at other people. But you got a taste of your own medicine tonight, eh? You finally found out what everyone thinks of you, eh? Well, maybe I'm fat, Hosanna, but at least I still grab 'em!

HOSANNA:

He still grabs them! He still grabs them alright! In the dark, yeah! In the meat-racks, yeah! In the parks, in the back alleys, at the movies! In the toilets! Oh, it's true, Cuirette, you used to be good-looking once, but now, now, you're nothing but a washroom cowboy . . . .

CUIRETTE:

I don't have to go there, you know. I do it for kicks.

HOSANNA:

Then where did you meet your Reynalda? Wasn't it at night? It couldn't have been during the daytime! I'll bet she doesn't have a clue what you really look like. Oh, how I'd love to be a little birdie, so I could fly over to Sandra's and peek in the window, just to see Reynalda's face when she finally gets a good look at you.

55

CUIRETTE:

I met Reynald on the street in the middle of the day, Hosanna. And, by the way, it could be a lot more serious than you think . . . .

HOSANNA:

If you're trying to scare me, dear . . . .

CUIRETTE:

I'm not trying to scare you. I'm just clueing you in. I might stay away longer than you think, you know . . . .

HOSANNA:

And what are you gonna do for money? You can't even buy gas . . . .

Pause.

Eh? . . . . You know I don't believe you, Cuirette. Okay, beat it. You've kept her waiting long enough. If you don't get your ass moving she's going to find someone else . . . I'm giving you three days off. Then you can come back and cook my meals . . . . That's all you're good for anyway . . . .

CUIRETTE:

That's all I'm good for, eh? That's not what you say at night . . . .

HOSANNA:

What I say at night, my friend, or if you prefer, whatever noises I make while we're pretending to fuck, believe me, they're just my way of trying to convince myself I'm enjoying it. What we do together, Cuirette, for a long time, it's been nothing more than . . . biology. I suppose you think your way of making love is pleasant for a . . . .

56

HOSANNA stops suddenly.

CUIRETTE:

For a woman . . . . Stopped yourself just in time, eh? You know, Hosanna, everytime you play the queen, or whenever you're trying to be funny, and especially when you're trying to get your hooks into some new biker, since that's what you dig most, you're always a woman. And everybody's gotta know it. Even when we come back here, and I'm tired and you're horny - and don't give me that shit about not enjoying it, Hosanna, 'cause you love it so much you can't get enough - when you're horny and I'm not - yeah, when I'm the one who doesn't want it - you launch into the same routine, prancing around, wiggling your ass, soaking yourself in that piss you call perfume, just to get me all worked up . . . but if we start fighting, or try to talk serious, you don't know what you are. You don't know if you're a man or a woman, Hosanna. You know it's stupid to call yourself a woman, 'cause I can throw it back in your face like I'm doing right now. And you know it's even stupider to try to act like a man when you're dressed in those rags, and you got that shit smeared all over your face . . . . So what are you, Hosanna? Eh? Would you mind telling me just what the fuck you are?

HOSANNA:

If I'm neither a man or a woman, then why do you stay with me? If you don't know what I am, who is it you go to bed with every night, the man or the woman? Answer me that, Cuirette, my pet. Is it my dresses that turn you on, or is it me? Is it Hosanna, the drag queen, or Claude, the farmer? If Hosanna turns you on, then why do you sleep with a guy? And if it's Claude, then why do you sleep with a guy *who looks like a woman?* Eh? It couldn't be that you're scared of women, could it?

CUIRETTE:

    I'm not scared of women.

HOSANNA:

    Listen, toughy, have you ever touched a woman? Oh,
    you look tough alright, but for four years, guess what,
    you've been my maid. You realize that? We've been
    together four years, and for four years I'm the boss.
    I'm the one who goes out to work, I'm the one who
    feeds you, and you're the one who washes the floors,
    does the dishes, and cooks the spaghetti. Do you
    realize that? Oh, you're always bragging about how you
    live off me, but do you ever tell anyone who does the
    laundry, who picks up the broken glass? Out there, you
    cruise around town on your bike, but when you're
    home, you scrub the pans, and you take out the garbage.
    Me, I'm a hairdresser by day, and a woman of the
    world by night . . . . But what are you? Huh? A cleaning
    lady who rides a motorcycle when she gets off work!

    Pause.

    You never thought of that, did you, that between the
    two of us, you're the woman. And you know what I
    am? I'm the man of the house, Cuirette. I'm the man.

CUIRETTE:

    That's bullshit! You're not the man of the house. You
    might give the orders, but you give them like a woman.

HOSANNA:

    But I still give the orders . . .

CUIRETTE:

    If you were a man, you'd act like a man, at least when
    you're alone. But no, when you're alone, you go on
    behaving exactly like a woman. You never act like a

man when you're anywhere near that goddamn mirror. And you sure as hell don't act like a man in bed . . . . Especially there! . . . . Yeah! In four years you haven't done one single thing in bed that would make me think you were a man, not one! You live like a woman, and you fuck like a woman. And ever since the lines started showing around your eyes and in the corners of your mouth, your pancake's getting thicker, just like a woman. You've even started wearing it to work, for Chrissake. You can't go out of the house in daylight without putting half a pound of shit on your face. You're getting old, Hosanna. You're getting old the way a woman gets old . . . . Fast! And it won't be long before you start getting all your crummy jokes about old queens right back in your face. It started tonight, and let me tell you, that's only the beginning. Just a few more wrinkles on your lovely puss, and then, believe me, baby, the fur's gonna start flying. They'll be taking chunks out of you . . . . The same treatment you've been giving them all these years.

Pause.

It's all over, Hosanna. After tonight, you're through playing the spring chicken.

He goes toward the door.

You hear me, Hosanna? After tonight you're through.

He opens the door.

And you want to know something really stupid?

Pause.

I love you, goddamn it. I love you!

He slams the door behind him. HOSANNA runs to the door and opens it, shouting.

HOSANNA:
Well you know, sometimes I'd like to fuck you, Cuirette! Sometimes I'd really like to fuck you!

She slams the door. She goes toward the bed and lights a cigarette. CUIRETTE's motorcycle can be heard driving away. HOSANNA runs to the window.

Blackout.

The sign on the Pharmacy continues to blink.

- *ACT TWO* -

*Half an hour later. HOSANNA, sitting up in bed is
smoking. She is still wearing her Cleopatra wig. The
urn-lamp is lit. The pharmacy sign suddenly goes off.
HOSANNA notices this right away, and turns her head
toward the window.*

HOSANNA: *putting out her cigarette*
Well, that takes care of that. No sleep tonight, Cinderella.

She puts the ashtray on the bedside table.

And I'm out of cigarettes. Shit! Everything happens to
me at once. Everything. Now if Cuirette were here,
he'd tell me in his big stupid voice, ''Cleopatra didn't
smoke, you know.'' For three weeks he's been driving
me nuts with his Cleopatra . . . . Well, you can't blame
him, can you? . . . . For the past three weeks I've been
driving him nuts with my goddamn costume.

''How do you know she didn't smoke? Listen, they
were all drug fiends, those Egyptians, the whole
goddamn bunch of them.''

Imitating CUIRETTE's voice.

''Like me, you mean?''

Her natural voice again.

"No, dear, not like you. They all made history."

CUIRETTE's voice.

"Yeah, well maybe you and me could make something else . . . ."

Natural voice.

"Shut up, dummy, you're getting on my nerves."

She gets out of bed.

Ladies and Gentlemen, you have just heard the fourteen thousand, two hundred and twelfth episode of our great love story, "Cuirette and Cleopatra," conceived, imagined, produced and *lived* by Claude Lemieux and Raymond Bolduc. Raymond Bolduc! Jesus, it should be against the law to call yourself Raymond Bolduc!

She looks at herself in the big mirror.

Some people, they have such ugly names they don't deserve to live. That's why actors and transvestites change their names. Because they-don't-deserve-to-live. Cha-cha-cha! A cigarette, a cigarette, my kingdom for a cigarette! Now who would give me a cigarette for this dump?

Silence.

My cheap little perfume factory, my two-bit whore house . . . . My God, it stinks in here. It's unbelievable how it stinks! But . . . the show must go on . . . and on . . . and on . . . and on . . . .

She goes to the vanity table.

Mirror, mirror, on the wall, who's the fairest of them all? Shut up!

She starts to laugh.

Oh well, La Duchesse . . . . She'll always be the funniest.

Long silence.

HOSANNA takes a jar of cream, then sets it back down again gently.

The telephone rings. HOSANNA turns and looks at it for a long while.

Good thing I wasn't asleep, eh?

She gets up slowly and answers the phone.

Hello, Genevieve Bujold!

She listens for a while without saying anything.

Sandra . . . Sandra, listen . . . . Of course I knew it was you, dear. Jeanne Moreau never calls me at this hour . . . . Listen, was it really all that funny tonight? Because if it wasn't, you know, I would appreciate it if you'd just bugger off . . . . Okay, please?

Silence.

Oh, it was that funny, was it? . . . . Then by all means, dear, keep it up. Keep it up!

She starts to hang up, then stops.

Oh, Sandra, you don't happen to have a cigarette, do you?

She starts to hang up again, but stops again.

Oh, by the way, Sandra, you got what you wanted,
Cuirette left half an hour ago, and he'll be there any
minute. So start playing with yourself, you fat pig. Start
working up a nice big hard on!

She hangs up.

Jesus, that woman gets on my tits!

*She goes back to the vanity table, takes the chair,
carries it downstage centre and sets it down, back to the
audience. She sits down, straddling the back of the chair.*

Two months ago, on one of those fabulous Friday nights
when we were all lying around Sandra's club, and we
were all plastered because we hadn't picked up any
tricks . . . . One of those really fabulous Friday nights
that might just as well have been a Thursday night, or a
Tuesday night, or a Saturday night, but which this time
happened to be a Friday night, Sandra plugged in the
microphone . . . . Now, there was no show that night,
so everything was unplugged, especially us girls, if you
get my drift? . . . . Anyway, Sandra plugged in the mike
to announce her annual Halloween party, her annual
costume bash that costs you an arm and a leg and only
buys you a lot of shit . . . . Now, I couldn't figure out
why she was using the mike because she'd just finished
telling us all about her party, going around to all
tables . . . . So I figured she was just making it
"official." Well, how stupid can you get! Then she told
us with that big smile of hers . . . the filthy bitch! I
should have known something was wrong! I should have
known!

Slowly.

She told us that this year the party was going to have a definite theme . . . . Now, she never mentioned anything about that before . . . . A definite theme that everyone would have to follow . . . . So up got La Duchesse, and between a few mouthfulls of scotch proposed we should all dress up like men and once and for all give ourselves a really good scare . . . . Me too, I thought that was funny as hell, but Cuirette . . . Cuirette jumped up and shoved La Duchesse back into her chair . . . . And then . . . .

Silence.

Then Sandra told us that the theme we had to follow for our costumes was - are you ready for this - famous women of history! And I fell for it! Christ, I walked straight into the trap.

Silence.

But how could I have known they hated me so much? Me! My heart was in my mouth. I was all goose bumps. Jesus, my big chance. My big chance had finally come! Cuirette, the gazelle, comes leaping over to my table . . . . "Did you hear that, Hosanna, did you hear?" The bastard! Probably winking at Sandra like a goddamned flashlight. And me, so excited I didn't even notice! Then La Duchesse stood up and shouted, "Hey, Hosanna, don't forget to ask Elizabeth Taylor if you can borrow her diamond, eh?" Everybody laughed. Me too. I was so happy. God, was I happy! Babalu was already talking about coming as Scheherazade, Candy-Baby as Marilyn Monroe, and we all know who Brigitte was thinking of, don't we? . . . But there wasn't one person, not one, who dared mention Elizabeth Taylor.

Silence.

Because Elizabeth Taylor . . . is mine! And they know it! Elizabeth Taylor's been mine for twenty years. The first movies I ever saw were Elizabeth Taylor movies. And the last movies I'm ever going to see will be Elizabeth Taylor movies. And someday, when I'm old-old-old, and rich-rich-rich, I'm going to buy me a movie projector that will run nonstop, and I'll sit and I'll watch Elizabeth Taylor make her entrance into Rome until I croak.

Silence.

I've drooled over Elizabeth Taylor, I've jerked off over Elizabeth Taylor! I've laughed like an idiot, I've bawled like a baby over Elizabeth Taylor, and I'll go on doing it over Elizabeth Taylor until I drop! I even skipped school to see Elizabeth Taylor make her entrance into Rome. And I'll sell my last false tooth, if I have to, to see her do it again!

She laughs.

Long silence.

She shrugs her shoulders.

Shit! What a pile of shit! Until now I was perfectly happy just to look at Elizabeth Taylor. I never let myself try to look like her . . . . At least not in front of other people . . . . Not yet . . . I wasn't ready yet! I wasn't deserving enough. Fuck me! Deserving enough! Me, Claude Lemieux, coiffeuse at la Plaza St. Hubert, I thought that someday I'd deserve to look like Elizabeth Taylor. And now . . . Christ!

Silence.

She closes her eyes.

There were at least . . . . Oh, at least two hundred thousand people, I think . . . . Oh, yes. At least two hundred thousand! Dressed all in different colours, on a set three miles long, with papier mache sphynxes, houses, temples, ruins, *doors*, yes, doors two hundred feet high, all made out of papier mache . . . . The crowd was roaring, dancing, screaming . . . . The papier mache doors opened, like gigantic church doors . . . . And thousands, millions of coloured birds that don't even shit went flying over the papier mache set . . . . Huge black slaves, their bodies glistening, lifted the chair onto their shoulders. The trumpets blared, the drums rolled, the sky . . . .

Silence.

The sky was wine red, and streaked with gold, Christ! And . . . Hosanna made her entrance! Hosanna, borne aloft in her chair, her chair suspended on a double axle to keep her level, dressed like Elizabeth Taylor, in her hands a whip and a golden ball of papier mache; Hosanna was making her entrance into Rome! And all the while, the sign from the Pharmacie Beaubien was flashing its red and yellow lights in the mirror, and Cuirette was snoring . . . .

Silence.

The sign from the Pharmacie Beaubien flashed its red and yellow lights in the mirror while Cuirette snored . . . . His arm around Hosanna as she made her triumphal entrance into Rome!

HOSANNA opens her eyes, gets up and looks again for a cigarette.

Hey, doesn't anybody have a cigarette, for Chrissake?

67

She sits down again.

There were at least . . . . At least twenty five
thousand extras, ... All dressed in the most fabulous
costumes! I've never seen such fabulous costumes! . . . .
And the set! God, it wasn't a set. It was a real city
made out of real marble. They built a real city out of
real marble with sphynxes and pyramids made of
stones! The biggest, most beautiful set I ever saw.
And the noise! Listen, they were screaming so loud, I
thought my ears were going to burst. Then the
procession began. Soldiers in chariots, real chariots,
soldiers on foot, real soldiers too, you know why?
Because they marched in perfect formation. Bands,
marching bands, and all the girls, made up to their
assholes, throwing real petals from real roses as if their
lives depended on it, doing belly dances and you name
it. Elephants . . . . Yes, there were even real
elephants! Then the marble doors, the real marble
doors opened wide and the crowd exploded . . . .

Silence.

HOSANNA trembles slightly.

. . . And Elizabeth Taylor made her entrance! Borne
aloft in her chair, her chair suspended on a double axle
to keep her level, Elizabeth Taylor, the real Elizabeth
Taylor - the one who started out in a dog show and
who's going to end up to be the richest bitch in the
world, with a diamond collar around her neck - the real
Elizabeth Taylor, not the papier mache one, made her
entrance into Rome, her arms folded across her real
breasts, loaded with jewels, a serpent around her head,
more beautiful . . . Jesus, more beautiful than Elizabeth
Taylor in Cleopatra . . . .

Silence.

And, I said to myself: one day, one day, you'll make your entrance too! Oh, it won't be much compared to that one, but it will be better than nothing . . . . And every drag queen in Montreal is going to shit blood!

Silence.

Well, my entrance . . . into Rome . . . .
Silence.

WHO WAS IT THAT SHIT BLOOD, EH? WHO SHIT BLOOD!

Silence.

Three weeks, three whole weeks of my life wasted preparing for a flop! Three weeks of hysteria, three weeks of frazzled nerves, three weeks of charging all over the city getting this junk together, all the special creams and pancakes, the eyeliners, the fabrics, the jewellery and all the other shit. Yes, shit! Three whole weeks to think up, design, "create" . . . .

She jumps up, goes to the closet and takes out the dress.

. . . To "create" that! That! That worthless piece of shit! I designed it myself! I cut it out myself! I stitched and hemmed the motherfucker, and I put every pearl and sequin on it with my very own lily-white hands. And I wore the thing, in person! I've been dreaming of this goddamn dress for ten years . . . . And what's worst of all, what's worst of all, this is exactly the way I imagined it! Yesterday, I thought my dress was beautiful. Yesterday I thought it was even better than the one I'd been dreaming of.

She throws the dress on the floor.

If only I hadn't been so proud of the thing! If I hadn't been so pleased with my face! But Christ, I was pleased with everything. *Yesterday . . . I was sure I was beautiful!* Yesterday . . . Hosanna was finally ready to make her entrance into Rome.

She calms herself a little.

The taxi driver couldn't believe it . . . my God, it's Elizabeth Taylor! You should have seen his eyes pop when I told him where I was going . . . . "Oh, come off it, you mean you're not a real woman! I don't believe it, I don't believe it!" And everytime he stopped for a red light, people pointed at the window, saying "Look, it's Elizabeth Taylor, it's Elizabeth Taylor!" And then, when I got to the club . . . .

Long silence.

When I got to the club and started up the stairs . . . .

She screams.

Why is it always so perfect in my mind?

She takes her dress in her arms and sits down again.

Of course I didn't sleep a wink all night. I kept telling myself, "Sleep, sleep, sleep, you've got to sleep, you'll have bags under your eyes." But . . . I couldn't sleep . . . I was dreaming! The drums were beating, and . . . .

Silence.

I watched Cuirette sleeping. He's beautiful when he's asleep. I didn't go to work. I told them I had a migraine. Shit, I hope Peter didn't singe my Jewish ladies.

Silence.

I started to get ready at eleven in the morning. No kidding. I took a bath and I gave myself the works. Beauty balls, bath salts, olive oil, vinegar, beer, egg yolks, you name it. When I got out of there I looked like an angel food cake.

She smiles.

It was Cuirette who said that. I dried myself from head to toe, every corner. There wasn't a square inch of me that wasn't completely new! Cuirette wanted . . . Cuirette wanted to rape me on the spot . . . . "You don't stink anymore," he kept telling me. "You don't stink!" Of course, I had my fun with him, eh? . . . I started parading up and down in the nude. "Baby, you gotta be dry, you gotta be dry, dry, dry, so the new, new, clothes you're going to wear, and the lovely paint job you're going to put on, don't pick up dirt or sweat. Baby, you gotta be clean! Virgin material! Untouched. Like Mary . . . the mother of God!" I looked at myself in the mirror . . . . Front view, profile, the back . . . . Oh, to be a swan! . . . . I almost broke my neck doing that . . . I'm still pretty ripe . . . . A bit big maybe. I mean, *statuesque*, but the proportions are good. Bloody good!

Silence.

That afternoon, about three o'clock, when I sat down to do my make-up . . . .

She puts the dress down, takes the chair, and goes to the vanity table.

I froze. Make that look like Elizabeth Taylor? My heart was beating so fast, I thought it was going to explode. But I said to myself, "Hosanna, it's now or never."

She gently picks up a jar of base make-up.

Slowly I picked up the first jar . . . I was trembling a bit . . . then . . . .

She flings the jar to the floor.

Even if I had been beautiful, it wouldn't have changed a thing. Being beautiful wasn't the problem. That had nothing to do with it. What they did to me had nothing to do with being beautiful. Okay, it's true. I got ahead in this town by being a bitch. So what . . . I only did what everyone else does. It's just that I've got more talent for it than the others, that's all. I've got a big mouth, and I like to shit on people. I always have and I always will. So what? The ones who get the shit, deserve the shit, everytime!

Pause.

That's not true, Hosanna. You shit on people whether they deserve it or not . . . . Anything for a laugh . . . . Well, what the hell, if you don't look after yourself in this town, you'll end up in a dark corner, sitting on your meat like the rest of the wallflowers. Thanks, but no thanks! I didn't crawl out of Ste-Eustache with my tail between my legs to eat a dog's dinner in Montreal. My big mouth, that's all I ever had. Can I help it if it made me famous? Now I'm not saying I've got the biggest yap in Montreal, 'cause that's not true. I can think of lots of people who could outdo me anytime, like that fat pig Sandra, for instance. But it won't be long before . . . .

She stops suddenly and comes back to sit downstage, bringing her chair with her.

At first I just watched La Duchesse and Sandra at work. I studied every move they made. I saw how they'd watch everyone else, then shit on them, smack them on the ass, stick out their tongues, tear off their wigs and their false eyelashes, and . . . I learned. I studied everything. I remembered everything. They thought I was some poor little Orphan Annie come to seek her fortune in the big city, and that the big city would squash her like a little bird, but they were wrong. Jesus, were they wrong! Then when I managed to lay my hands on . . . . My hands. That's one way of putting it . . . . When I managed to get my hooks into Cuirette, Sandra, who'd had her eye on him for a long time, finally deigned to notice me, the bitch, at which point I told her to go jerk off with a handful of thumbtacks. And that's when Sandra learned who I was. And that's when Montreal learned to respect me! That's when I opened my big yap and started to talk back. There's nothing I wouldn't say, nothing I wouldn't do, to keep my hands on Cuirette, and everyone else's off. Oh, maybe Sandra owned the joint, and maybe La Duchesse was the queen of queens on the Main, but Hosanna was fixing her sights. Hosanna was preparing her entrance.

She stops suddenly and starts trembling like a leaf.

Still, I got to be friends with La Duchesse . . . . during one of her endless fights with Sandra . . . . And . . . . Shut up, Hosanna, shut up. Everything's finished . . . . Everything's fucked, the whole thing is fucked!

A very long silence.

It took me at least three hours to get enough shit on
my face to look just a little bit like something that
might vaguely resemble, from a distance, Elizabeth
Taylor in Cleopatra . . . . Then the wig, which, by the
way, took me two weeks to talk a client into loaning
me, I put on the wig . . . and I looked exactly the way
I look right now . . . minus what got washed away in
the flood, of course. I put on the sequins, one by one,
I put on the eyelashes, one by one . . . . It's the only
way to do it, eh? . . . . I redid my beauty spot ninety-
three-and-a-half times and I moved it twenty-six times
because where Elizabeth Taylor's got hers doesn't look
good on me . . . but of course I wound up putting it in
the same place as hers . . . . For once Cuirette didn't
laugh . . . . He watched me very seriously . . . Christ,
if I'd known, if I'd even suspected, I'd have taken my
nail file and shiskebobbed his two eyeballs. He must
have been killing himself all day long trying to keep a
straight face . . . . Anyway, by six o'clock I was ready
for my dress, but the party wasn't till midnight. So I
sat myself down, turned on the TV, and from six till
eleven-thirty I didn't budge. For five-and-a-half hours I
watched the CBC girls do their numbers, right to the
bitter end of "Appelez-moi, Lise." But then when they
tried to stick me with a re-run of "La Symphonie
Pastorale" with Michelle Morgan and Pierre Blanchard,
I said, "Cuirette, that's it! Get me my dress, my big
moment has come!" He helped me to get dressed the
bastard. He even did up my hooks. He even had the
nerve to tell me I didn't look too bad. And, I took it as
a compliment! Finally when everything was . . . strapped
into place . . . I closed my eyes and stood in front of
the mirror . . . . Then, I looked. And that's when it hit
me smack in the face. Cuirette was behind me . . . I
saw him smiling in the mirror . . . . And I knew . . . I

knew I shouldn't be going to that goddamn party. And suddenly I didn't want to go anymore! I didn't want to go, but . . . I looked at myself . . . *and I thought I was beautiful!* JESUS CHRIST! JESUS, JESUS, MOTHERFUCKING CHRIST!

Silence.

I told Cuirette to call me a taxi . . . I asked him if he was coming with me or if he was going to take his bike . . . . He told me he'd rather take his bike and get there ahead of me so he could see me arrive. Jesus, I was so blind, it's unbelievable, so fucking blind! As soon as he called the taxi, he was out the door . . . . Wait, that's not true . . . . He stood there for a minute . . . . He stood there staring at me with this funny look on his face . . . and I thought he was going to say something nice! After that, he left . . . . The door slammed, the bike roared off, and that was that! The taxi arrived . . . I went downstairs . . . . When I got in the car, the driver took one look at me and said, "Yeah, I know, you're going to Sandra's drag party." I was the fourth one he'd taken over there that night. People did not stop at every light and say, "Look, it's Elizabeth Taylor, it's Elizabeth Taylor!" But that didn't matter . . . . It was dark in the car . . . .

Silence.

All of a sudden, I got scared again. My teeth were shaking, my knees were shaking, my balls were shaking . . . . *And before I knew it, we'd arrived at Sandra's club.*

The door opens slowly and CUIRETTE walks in.

CUIRETTE: *after a long silence*
I didn't go to Sandra's party . . . .

HOSANNA: *after a silence*
Cuirette was waiting for me at the door with . . . .

CUIRETTE: *a little louder*
I didn't go to the party . . . .

HOSANNA:
. . . . With La Duchesse . . . dressed as a man!

CUIRETTE:
I went for a ride instead . . . .

HOSANNA:
I should have stayed in the car! I should have stayed
there and locked the door when I saw La Duchesse
dressed as a man on Halloween. Right there I should
have understood everything.

CUIRETTE:
. . . . In Parc Lafontaine. I went back to Parc Lafontaine.

HOSANNA:
The first thing I saw when we turned to corner was
Cuirette with La Duchesse.

CUIRETTE:
Nobody there.

HOSANNA:
Dressed as a man.

Silence.

Nothing moves.

CUIRETTE:

I checked every path, made as much noise as I could, yelled my head off.

HOSANNA:

When I got out of the taxi, La Duchesse came charging over, but Cuirette wouldn't let her speak to me. She started yelling, but she was so drunk I couldn't tell what she was saying . . . .

CUIRETTE:

They've fucked me, Hosanna! They've really fucked me up!

HOSANNA:

If La Duchesse had been able to warn me, none of this would have happened!

CUIRETTE:

I don't like it when things change. "You bastards, you've gone and changed it, eh, you've changed it all around! You pigs! You're scared they'll be a few dark corners left, eh, so you put your fuckin' lights up all over the place! Well, tough shit! From now on we'll do it right under your noses!" I'm telling you, Hosanna, if I'd seen a cop I woulda run him down. "From now on we're gonna do it in public, goddamn it! And if there's lots of fags who ride bikes, there's just as many fags in the fuckin' police force, and that's a fact! So why don't we do it together, eh! We'll all get under the lights, drop our pants, and go to it right in the middle of the fuckin' baseball field!"

Silence.

If I'd seen a cop . . . I probably would have run like hell, as usual . . . .

77

Silence.

The bastards have changed everything, Hosanna! Even
Parc Lafontaine . . . .

Silence.

This is the only place I know where nothing changes.
The only place where time just stops . . . . You
know? . . . I don't want things to change!

Very softly.

You know what I mean?

HOSANNA:
I tell you, the receiving line was a bit sparse. No
fanfares, no extras . . . . When I started up the stairs
my balloon was already half-popped.

CUIRETTE:
I didn't think it'd go that far . . . .

HOSANNA:
The further I got up the stairs, the more I could feel
something was wrong . . . then all of a sudden I heard
La Duchesse scream, "Don't go in, Hosanna, don't go in!"

CUIRETTE:
It wasn't my fault . . . .

HOSANNA:
I didn't even have to open the door . . . . It opened by
itself . . . . It was a little darker than usual, I couldn't
see what was going on . . . I went in . . . I went in,
goddamn it, I went in!

CUIRETTE:

I almost told you before I left, but . . . everything was ready . . . and . . . I thought . . . . Shit, I didn't think they'd go that far . . . .

HOSANNA:

Then the lights went on, every light in the place . . . . For a second I thought they had a nice surprise for me . . . . Oh, they had a surprise alright . . . . But it wasn't quite what I had in mind . . . .

CUIRETTE:

They didn't tell me they were going to go that far, Hosanna.

HOSANNA:

Everybody . . . was dressed . . . like Elizabeth Taylor in "Cleopatra."

Long Silence.

CUIRETTE:

Sandra just said that . . . .

Very long silence.

It's awful, Hosanna, they've stuck their lights all over the place.

HOSANNA:

The whole gang! Every single one! Babalu, Candy, Mimi, Lolita, Brigitte, Carole, and . . . Sandra! Every bitch in the place! And every one of them dressed better than me! Every one made up better than me!

Pause.

I looked like a beggar!

Pause.

They all acted as if nothing was wrong . . . . Me
too . . . I acted as if nothing was wrong. Jesus, I felt
my whole body was exploding. I felt like I was falling
into a pit. I could hardly breathe, for Chrissake! But I
didn't flinch. I just stood there staring into the room.

*Throughout the following two speeches, both characters
speak at once, in the same tone, at the same speed. It
is not important that one be heard more than another.
CUIRETTE speaks to HOSANNA, but HOSANNA
does not listen and talks to herself.*

CUIRETTE:
They just said they wanted to play a joke on
you . . . 'cause you've gotten to be such a pain in the
ass . . . . And you've been giving me a pain in the ass
too, Hosanna. I'm sick to death of your stupid games,
and your smart-ass remarks, and your goddamn scenes
that never end . . . I thought they just wanted
to . . . teach you a lesson . . . I let Sandra drag me
into it . . . . You know what she's like . . . . And . . . .
Well, it was fun getting everything ready with her,
Hosanna . . . . We'd worked it all out, every detail.
There was no way it wasn't going to work . . . . And it
did work . . . And I laughed when I saw you arrive
with your nose in the air, so sure of yourself in your
cheap little outfit . . . And I laughed when you went in
there and they turned on the lights . . . I laughed at
everything, Hosanna, I laughed at everything . . . .
Because I hated you! If you only knew how much I've
hated you these last few months! But now . . . I see
what they've done to you, Hosanna . . . .

HOSANNA:
I could have strangled them all with my bare hands! I

could have skinned them alive, the bitches! But I said to myself, "Hang on, Hosanna, get a hold of yourself. You've got to act like nothing's happened. If you do anything, you'll only make it worse." I was standing in the door, and no one was looking at me. But I could feel everyone watching me out of the corner of their eyes to see what I was going to do. Everyone was waiting for me to turn away so they could look at me. They were all waiting for me to crack, to collapse on the floor yelling and screaming. But I didn't . . . I just stood there. And I wasn't looking at anyone either. I was looking at the mirror ball that had just started turning, pouring splotches of red and yellow light on my face. Red and yellow lights!

Silence.

Hosanna had made her entrance into Rome, and everyone was dressed like her! Only better!

Silence.

CUIRETTE:
I don't know how to tell you this . . . .

HOSANNA:
Slowly I walked into the room full of Cleopatras. I sat down at my usual table. The waiter, who was all decked out in some kind of white toga, came over with a drink . . . . He said it was the evening special, "The Cleopatra Special!" Brigitte burst out laughing at the table next to me. Carole poked her one to shut her up. I drank my "Cleopatra Special." It was ginger ale.

Pause.

And then Cuirette . . . Cuirette came over and sat down in front of me with a big smile on his face.

HOSANNA looks at CUIRETTE for the first time since he came in.

Cuirette, have you got a cigarette? I'm dying!

CUIRETTE takes out a pack of cigarettes, takes one out, gives it to HOSANNA and lights it. Then he goes behind HOSANNA and puts his hands on her shoulders. He will stay like that until the end of HOSANNA's monologue.

Sandra, who by the way, makes a very fat Cleopatra, climbed up on the stage to get her show rolling. The same stupid jokes: "Good evening, Ladies and Gentlemen, and others . . . ." The same boring crap she's been dishing up for years . . . followed by the same boring songs she's been trying to sing for years . . . . People laughed, as usual, in the same spots, as usual . . . . But, I was looking at you, Cuirette. And you were doing everything you could to avoid looking at me. Oh, you were having a ball. You could hardly wait. You could hardly wait for the fat pig to call out my name so I'd have to go up on that stage and show off my rags!

Pause.

When she announced that the contest was going to start, I nearly had a hemorrhage. I wanted to throw my second ginger ale right in your face, just to make you look at me . . . and then to get out, out, out! But no! I had to stay. I had to prove . . . that I'm strong, that I don't care about all your stupid jokes. I had to show them that Hosanna can take it, and that she's not just anybody! If you only knew, Raymond.

Pause.

82

They started with Bambi. Of course all her friends thought she was fabulous. I watched her. She was beautiful. Next, it was Candy's turn. Now Candy's a real dog, eh, but for once . . . she almost made it. They were cheering and whistling . . . . The third Cleopatra was Carole. With a full length dress it was almost bearable, considering her legs don't grow in the same direction. After that . . . my turn. I don't know if you've ever heard a silence like that, Cuirette . . . I know I haven't. When Sandra called, or rather screamed my name, you'd have thought someone had cut off the sound. For a second I sat there nailed to my chair . . . I think I was already dead. Then I don't know who, but someone began to shout, "Hosanna, Hosanna, Hosanna, Ho!" Then they all started banging their tables, yelling, "Hosanna, Hosanna. Come on, Liz, strut your stuff!" You were laughing so hard, Cuirette. You were laughing so hard, it was you that made me decide to go up on that stage! So I got up . . . and I climbed the three steps, everyone shouting, "Hosannna, Hosanna," all around me . . . . And right there, in the middle of the stage, with everyone laughing at me, and whistling, and calling me stupid names, I said to myself, "Cleopatra is a pile of shit! Elizabeth Taylor is a pile of shit! You asked for your pile of shit, Hosanna-de-Ste-Eustache. Well, here it is. Your big pile of shit!" Now listen, Cuirette, I wasn't Cleopatra anymore I was Sampson, do you hear me? Sampson! And right there, I completely destroyed my papier mache set! Because you had completely destroyed my papier mache life.

Pause.

I never knew you all hated me so much . . . .

HOSANNA puts her head against CUIRETTE's stomach.

I'm a man, Raymond. If I ran out of there like that, tumbling down the stairs almost breaking my bloody neck, if I ran out, Raymond, it's because . . . I'm not a woman . . . . And you're going to have to get used to that . . . .

Silence.

Complete change of tone.

Why didn't you go to the party?

CUIRETTE:
I didn't feel like it . . . . Anyway, you're the one who sent me . . . .

HOSANNA:
And Reynalda?

CUIRETTE:
Reynalda can find someone else.

HOSANNA:
So she really does exist?

CUIRETTE:
Of course she does.

HOSANNA:
Ohh, it's not like you to let go of an easy catch . . . .

CUIRETTE:
I'll find her again . . . . You're not in bed yet?

HOSANNA:
I was a while ago, but I couldn't sleep . . . .

CUIRETTE:
No wonder, with all that crap on your face . . . .

HOSANNA:
I didn't feel like taking it off.

CUIRETTE:
It's hot in here . . . .

HOSANNA:
Open the window . . . .

CUIRETTE:
We'll freeze . . . .

HOSANNA:
Then don't complain . . . .

> *HOSANNA gets into bed. CUIRETTE starts getting undressed.*

The stink doesn't bother you?

CUIRETTE: *slight pause*
What stink?

HOSANNA:
I guess I can sleep now . . . .

CUIRETTE:
Now that I'm back . . . .

HOSANNA: *slight pause*
Yes, now that you're back.

CUIRETTE:
Hosanna . . . .

HOSANNA:
What . . . .

CUIRETTE:
What about your mother?

HOSANNA:
What about her?

CUIRETTE:
Is she really coming?

HOSANNA:
Of course she is.

CUIRETTE:
What are we gonna do?

HOSANNA:
She can sleep on the floor . . . . Come on . . . .

CUIRETTE:
Hosanna . . . .

HOSANNA:
What! . . . .

CUIRETTE:
I guess there's no point in saying I'm sorry . . . .

HOSANNA:
You're right . . . .

   CUIRETTE gets into bed.

CUIRETTE:
You know . . . . Ah, I can't seem to tell you anything